LIFE at the 50 YARD LINE

John Gondeck

ISBN 978-1-63630-840-1 (Paperback)
ISBN 978-1-63630-841-8 (Digital)

Covenant Books, Inc.
11661 Hwy 707
Murrells Inlet, SC 29576
www.covenantbooks.com

THE PLAYERS

Owner: God
Co-Owners: Jesus (the Son) and Holy Spirit
Head Coach: Jesus the Intercessor (our advocate)
Line Coach: the Holy Spirit
Offensive and defensive co-coordinators: pastors and teachers

Offensive Line

Quarterback
Center
Right tackle
Left tackle
Tight end
Fullback
Halfback
Two Wide receivers
Left guard
Right guard
Referees
Athletic trainer
Water boys

Defensive Line

Three Linebackers
Two Defensive tackles
Two Defensive ends
Two Cornerbacks
Two Safeties

THE GAME

Four Quarters
One hundred yards
The bench
Coin toss
Kickoff
The run
The tackle
Huddle
The pass
Halftime
Back to the game
Two-minute warning
Game over

INTRODUCTION

Where does life truly begin and where will it take us? Everyone starts somewhere. When will we reach the halfway point? Just maybe, we have passed it. Unlike those who play football, we can't see our own fifty-yard line. We know that it is out there somewhere, but where? Have we passed it, or are we approaching it? Or, just possibly, are we standing on it? These are questions that may never be answered. Our parents make plans and dream dreams for us, and we, in turn, make plans for our children. However, God has His plans for us as well. "For I know the thoughts that I think toward you, says the Lord, thoughts of peace and not of evil, to give you a future and a hope."

After writing two books and having them published (which I would never have thought I would be doing), I was taking a walk one morning when the title of this book came to mind. I know that it was not of me, but God inspired me because I am not a football person. I do like the playoffs, and that is about all. And yet as I was thinking on the title and of life itself, I started to ponder over my own life. Where am I? When my coin was tossed and I chose to receive, did my game begin then, or had I been playing for some time and never realized it? There are people who are very important to the game yet very seldom are noticed, and so it is in life. There are so many participants who affect our everyday lives that we hardly take notice. We take notice to our immediate family, those who we live with, but what about those who we come in contact with on a daily basis?

Have you ever found yourself going in a direction that you were not intending to go? What or who prompted you to make the change? Just like in football, if a block in front of you happened, you

7

would immediately change direction, or you might want to change direction if someone was coming straight at you. In life, there are many unseen forces that affect our lives moment by moment of every day.

Years ago, when my wife and I were looking to move, our eyes were set toward Carroll County, Maryland. However, that was not God's plan. His direction brought us to Caroline County, Maryland. A new course was charted, and a different lifestyle began. Life is always made up of choices, and as I told my children, you can make good choices, and you can make bad choices. Either way, you have to live with them until you make another change.

Football is one of those sports where there are many people making the decisions as to what is to take place on the field with the goal of winning the game. The game of life is similar in many ways. There may be a parent or spouse who calls the shots for you, giving you guidance, which could be good or bad. There could also be a friend or boss giving you direction, and just possibly, you have that inner drive or ambition, even greed, that drives you on. The possibility of yet another influence in your life to help you make good sound decisions could be just a whisper away. You will find yourself playing offense sometimes and defense at other times. There are times when you will find yourself playing many different positions throughout the game. Finally, the day comes when you find your place and you become very comfortable in it. So that you don't get too comfortable, change comes, and some change is good. Strength and growth come from change as long as it is in a positive direction.

Rick Kollinger said it well, "Knowing the positions in football is very important because it will help you better understand the announcers and what is occurring on the field. Many of the TV announcers are ex-players and coaches so they need to make the plays sound extremely complicated in order to justify their salaries." This is happening not just in the world of football but also in the game of life. How many times have we seen someone with little to no experience take charge of a corporation, small business, or even the presidency and try to make what they do sound extremely hard or complicated in order to justify the fanfare? Life can be short no matter what position you play. You may be in the game for just a short time or for the whole game. The most important thing to remember is this: Play the game with all that is within you. Play the game with the skills that you have. Learn all you can. Put to use your knowledge, wisdom, understanding, and experience; and let these things promote you to the next level. Proverbs 4:7 says, "Wisdom is the principal thing, therefore, get wisdom and in all you're getting get understanding also." Play fair even when your opponent doesn't. The war has been won even though the battles go on.

CHAPTER 1

The Owners

Every team starts with an owner or multiple owners, and they make the decisions on who will play and who will not and what their salaries will be. The cities where these teams are located have put together many attractive financial packages to lure the teams into their area. These are multimillion-dollar deals with negotiations going on well into the midnight hour. For Baltimore, it was a $200 million, rent-free stadium and $80 million personal seat license fee. So every team negotiates their own packages to move or to stay. Plans for how and where the stadium would be built, the parking, the vendors, and the splits would be worked out over time so that everyone would benefit financially. Calculations for seating, how many people can be expected, box seats, upper and lower sections, and the cost per seat per section all the way up to what is known as the nosebleed section are taken into consideration. This is the section at the very top where, when looking down, the players look like ants. These seats, during the Super Bowl 2014, sold for nearly $5,000.

There are other considerations such as who will supply the vendors, the cost of goods, the commission split, and all those who will be bringing these goods to the fans. Stadium upkeep is just another factor that many of us forget. When you attend one of these games, remember that there is someone who cleaned the seats, swept the floors, cleaned the restrooms, and helped you find your seat. Let us not forget the cost of electricity for the lights, scoreboard, elevators, and escalators. Before you even get into the stadium, you need to find a parking spot. There you will find a myriad of people to help you find that spot of which you can't seem to find for some reason when the game is over. From there to the entrance gate, you will run a gauntlet of outside vendors, all vying for your money on peanuts and souvenirs.

In the beginning, God created…

The life of faith has two basic components, offensive and defensive, much like football. The believer in the offensive position needs to apply discipline to grow spiritually and win just like athletes do while preparing themselves for the game of football and the position they play. The big difference between those playing football and Christians on the field of life is that the Christians play both offensive and defensive positions. As an offensive player, we win others to Christ to be on His team. As a defensive player, we need to be on guard. We need to be on guard against false teachings, which can lead us astray. If you listen to your head instead of the coach, you could lose the game. It is written in 1 Peter 5:8–9 NKJV (New King James Version), "Be sober, be vigilant; because your adversary the devil walks about like a roaring lion, seeking whom he may devour. Resist him, steadfast in the faith…"

Have you ever thought about this? That football and the game of life are similar in many ways? Each team has at least one owner in the game and in life. The Ravens, for instance, is owned by Steve Bisciotti; and the life team is owned by El Elyon (God Most High), Jehovah, and Adonai. Steve graduated from Salisbury State in 1982 with a degree in liberal arts. He apparently did well during the next eighteen years. With hard work and negotiations, by March of 2000, he owned 49 percent of the team; and by 2004, he purchased the remaining 51 percent. His net worth is now $4.3 billion. However, there is no comparison between him and El Elyon. Jehovah has no beginning. He always was and always will be. He created *all* things, the heavens and the earth and *all* that is in them, the gold, the silver, and all creatures great and small on the earth, under the earth, and in the sea. He doesn't need to ask for anything. He owns it *all* and calls every star by name. So Adonai has no measurable net worth. He didn't attend college, for He is *all* wisdom and knowledge. You see, Mr. Bisciotti is limited on his game field by end zones. El Elyon has no limits on His field. The owners take everything into account before the game begins. Mr. Bisciotti has people looking at the books and has a pretty good idea of what the cost will be per game, including how much his share will be. Jehovah also knew the cost and was willing to pay the price to redeem His people, His creation. You see, no one could ever afford the price, no matter how rich they were, to redeem His creation—mankind. After the world was created, Adonai created mankind, and He gave it (the world) to Adam and Eve. They, in turn, gave it over to Lucifer by sinning against El Elyon (God Most High). So now, in the game of life, there are two owners. There is Jehovah, who cannot lose, and Lucifer, who lost at the cross and cannot win. When Lucifer left the realm of heaven, he took with him one-third of the angels, and together they have put together a team to disrupt the game of life for those on Adonai's side. Lucifer is a liar and always has been. He will mess with your head, your heart, your health, your family, your friends, your finances, and your life along with anything else that he can use to get you go against El Elyon. However, in every game, there is a head coach, and John Harbaugh is the head coach for the Ravens and has been since 2008, which should tell you that he is doing something right. Yeshua is the head coach for Jehovah's team and has been for over two thousand years. Quite a track record, wouldn't you say? He has never lost yet. Everyone who has called on Him has never been turned away. In the game of football, many times, teams are bought and sold like a commodity. Players are also sold and traded with the hope of making the team better. The owners are constantly looking to make a dollar. They may sell a team for profit or loss, depending on what their tax accountant says. Jehovah will never sell his team. He has already paid the ultimate price, and no one could ever pay more. No matter how good or bad you are, on or off the field, God will not let you go. You will never be traded. You see, in the game of football, the owners, the scouts, and the coaches look for how fast you can run and how quick you are able to move from side to side, backward, and forward. Can you actually catch a ball on the run? How are you built—tall, short, big, or small? And if you are going to be a guard, can you stand your ground? All these things are the outward appearance, yet El Elyon looks on the inside. He sees your heart.

Like in the movie *Rudy*, all the coaches looked at the outer appearance. Rudy was short and stocky, not much going for him, yet he had a heart for the game. So he cheered the team by giving encouragement to the players. The coach wouldn't put him in the game. He never let his discouragement show. He suited up every time there was a game just in case and was always waiting to hear, "Rudy, go out there and play." But it didn't happen. Finally, the time came. His team was in the biggest game of the season, and they were losing. Halftime came, and into the locker room, they went. They went over the plays. Rudy just kept asking to be put in the game, but the coach refused. At last, down to the last seconds of the game, the coach, seeing the discouragement on Rudy's face, said, "Rudy, go out there and take your position." With all the enthusiasm and energy he could muster, he ran onto the field. His heart was pounding so loud that the crowd caught the sound and cheered him on. The ball snapped, and with all that was inside him—blood pulsing through his veins, muscles being pushed to their limit—he ran and carried the ball over the goal line, scoring to win the game. It is what is on the inside of man that makes the difference.

A friend of mine, Roger Layton, was a top coach for the little league team in Denton. With all the kids who came before him over the years, only a few had a heart for the game, and he saw the inner person and encouraged them. If you have a heart toward God, He will take you to heights unknown. Men like Graham, Sunday, Luther, and King are just a few of the countless thousands to reach beyond what their mind could conceive. But they trusted in God, and He led them. Are you a "Rudy" in your church? Is it in your heart to get into the game of life within your church to do whatever the Lord would have you to do? Would you be a water boy, a floor scrubber, a duster, or a sweeper for Jesus? Many times, we need to start at a lowly position before the promotion comes. Learning how to be an encourager and a worker is all part of the process. God the Father, Jesus the Son, and the Holy Spirit are all co-owners of the family of God; and Jesus is the head coach. When you are born again into the family of God, you are given a gift or multiple gifts to be used for the kingdom of God. We will look at those in later chapters. The head coach makes many decisions from his experience and knowledge of the game, and with that, he plans to win, not lose. Many changes are made during the course of the game, and they are not always for the good. However, if you learn how to adjust to different situations as they come, you can still end up scoring.

I don't know how the coaches feel when they see grown men doing silly dances in the end zone after making a touchdown, but I would wonder about how many hours they spend with their buddies in the privacy of their own homes or the locker room, practicing their gyrations, backflips, and dance steps (which are better than the "Boot Scootin' Boogie"), even practicing their high jump just so they can spike a football over the goalpost. I guess all this is to show someone that they even look good when they lose.

However, in the game of life, the true head coach, Jesus (Yeshua), doesn't approve of such foolishness, for even He humbled Himself to be a servant. He teaches against pride and self-indulgence. All through the Scriptures, we see men who were puffed up because of all they owned only to see it taken away. We should not think so highly of ourselves that we become no earthly good for the team. There has been many a good player who was traded or let go because they saw themselves as better than everyone else, too good to be let go or traded. Shouldn't we be looking inside to see how our head coach sees us? How do we line up with what the Word says? Are we reading and studying every day the "manual" that should be guiding us, or are we happy to just look at it once a week? If any athlete only practiced once a week, they most likely would never play in the game. They would never suit up. They would never be rewarded. They would have no self-esteem and no outlandish paychecks. However, if they practice and exercise on a regular basis, they will be ready for the challenges ahead.

There is a plan book that the coach wants everyone to learn backward and forward. We need to know the various positions of the other players and what their functions are on the field. The plan book has each player's position noted, what happens after the ball is snapped, what each player is to do, and where they are to go.

There is also a plan book for Christians to follow, the Holy Bible, and if we follow the instructions laid out in it, we *will* win. Like the football players, we are instructed; however, unlike the football players, we are instructed to "go into the entire world and preach the gospel to every creature. He who believes and is baptized will be saved; but he who does not believe will be condemned. And these signs WILL follow those who believe; In My name they will cast out demons; they WILL speak with new tongues; they Will take up serpents and if they drink anything deadly, it Will by no means hurt them; they Will lay hands on the sick and they Will recover" Mark 16:15–18 (New King James Version). So our manual makes it pretty plain what we are to do for the team.

CHAPTER 2

Field Entry Position

The time has come for the teams to enter the field, and as the different players come onto the field, they are cheered by the waiting fans. Each team enters along with their respective coaches (the head coach and line coach), offensive and defensive coordinators, the athletic trainers, and the water boys. These are also known as pastors and teachers to the Christians. The coaches bring the team to a belief in themselves and in the coaches that they can win if they do what they are instructed to do and give it their all. The same holds true for pastors and teachers as they minister to a new convert (from an unbeliever to a believer). When a person is born again and becomes a believer, the angels in heaven rejoice. The pastors share the Word of God and, many times, share the part of a teacher to help the new Christian grow in the faith. There are those who have the gift of teaching called by God to fill that office, and then there are others who would like to be teachers but are not ready. The fifth chapter of Hebrews tells us, "For though by this time you ought to be teachers, you need someone to teach you again the first principals of the oracles of God and you have come to need milk and not solid food. For everyone who partakes only of milk is unskilled in the word of righteousness, for he is a baby. But solid food belongs to those who are of full age, that is, those who by reason of use have their senses exercised to discern both good and evil."

So you see, the field entry position is for the second-string and the unskilled. There are times when the second-string quarterback is called up to play due to an injury that took place on the field. Like Rudy, they have been waiting and training for this moment. This is not something that just happens by chance—that a quarterback who has no skills, no practice, and no knowledge of the game let alone knowledge of the various plays that need to be called is called off the bench. No, they need to be ready at all times for they do not know the time when they will be called up. The same holds true for a Christian. He must be ready, and that takes time. It doesn't happen overnight. Much time must be spent in reading the Word of God. Rehearsing the Word, committing the Word to memory, and settling the Word in your heart and in your mouth prepare you for the time when you have to give an account. 1 Peter 3:15–17 says, "But sanctify the Lord God in your hearts and always be ready to give a defense to everyone who asks you a reason for the hope that is in you with meekness and fear; have a good conscience, that when they defame you as evildoers, those who revile your good conduct in Christ may be ashamed. For it is better, if it is the will of God, to suffer for doing good than for doing evil." And then again, 2 Timothy 4:2 says, "Preach the word! Be ready in season and out of season. Convince, rebuke, exhort, with all longsuffering and teaching."

A rookie player may take a lot of hard knocks because there is a lot of learning that needs to take place before he gets to second or first string. Many preachers and teachers of the Word don't make it to second-string because the tests are too difficult. They don't have the stamina to stay in the fight. Positioning for the greatest impact is a hard road and can be long as well. However, we see people like Paul. All through the New Testament and the trials and tests that he was confronted with, he stood true to course, not wavering. And so it is with those who want to be a pro football player. It takes determination, stamina, a drive that comes from within, and a mindset that can't be shaken even in the face of adversity. The time for training the body comes with a price. Constant exercise is required. The body needs to react a certain way when the brain says to the body to do something that it is not used to doing. There is time spent in books, learning plays, hand signals, and calls. Are you being called to enter this game of life that is set before you? Are you willing to pay the price? Do you have that determination to go through all the trials that could come your way? Are you willing to learn all you can about the Word of God, which is God's playbook with all you need to know to be victorious in this life? You must spend time in the Word, not just reading but also meditating. In the book of Proverbs, it says that one who wins souls is wise. Jesus said that we would be fishers of men, and any good fisherman knows that you have many different lures in your box when you go fishing because all fish don't eat the same food. Not only is the bait important but also the time of day and the tide. The fifty-yard line of life, unlike the fifty-yard line in football, is not easily seen, if seen at all. Psalm 91 speaks of a long life, and I expect that unless the Lord's return for His church happens within the next forty-seven years. Otherwise, I plan to close my eyes on that day and leave my body and go home.

A rookie player is one who enters the game maybe as a child with a dream, hopefully his and not his parents. I remember seeing my grandsons starting out and all suited up with their football helmet, jersey, pants, and shoulder pads. They run out on the field, all excited and ready to do something, just don't know what. The coaches take time with small groups and try their best to explain what these little fellows are to do and how to do it. As time goes by, many will stop playing, and a few will continue on into high school and possibly college. Maybe one out of ten will actually be drafted. And so it is with the church family. Many will be called, but only a few will be chosen. With many who go into the ministry, they want to be recognized by everyone and get the applause, yet there are many who just want to be used by God. It doesn't matter if they are sweeping floors, washing dishes, or cleaning bathrooms just as long as they are doing for God and not man. God's Word says that if you will be faithful in the little things, He will reward you with bigger things. So we see many going to Bible college, coming out with a degree and big dreams only to find that it may not have been God's plan for their life. Looks can be deceiving. For instance, when you see TV evangelists and pastors of megachurches, you think that is what you would like to be a part of. The cost is many times beyond how much you may want to pay. For a child who is willing to go the distance, work out when they don't feel like it, study when their friends are going to the beach, or practice when their body says "I can't do any more," the rewards can be great. Billy Graham, chosen by God, spent many times away from family, stayed up late into the evening, and got up early to spend time alone with God. He traveled all over the world, preaching the gospel message, willing to pay the price that some may be saved. Yes, he was willing to do whatever was required of him to fulfill his calling. That's what it takes to be a champion.

There are many players mentioned throughout the Scriptures who have stories to share that would cause many to flee in fear. King David, as a boy, grew up taking care of sheep for the family and became very good with a sling since he had nothing else to do with his time. He did recognize that there was a God in heaven of whom he sang and prayed to. The time came when he faced a giant that came against Israel. He defeated him with a sling and a stone, for God was with him. How many times have you faced a giant in your life? Did you run in fear, or did you stand your ground with the Word of God? God picks the players for His team, and it is not by the outward appearance but by the heart. And then there was Joshua, trained under Moses and became a great leader leading the people into the promised land. Samson was a man of great strength, dedicated to God as a child, and his hair was never to be cut. In his death, he destroyed more of the enemy of Israel than during his life. Daniel, Shadrach, Meshach, and Abednego are others handpicked by God as His representatives. They withstood the lion's den, the fiery furnace, and several Persian kings.

The time has come when you are no longer a rookie and you move into second-string, getting some playing time. I know of a pastor who came to our church as a youth pastor, and then one Sunday morning, he brought the message. My wife said then that he was destined to have his own church. A few years went by, and he continued as associate pastor, all the time growing. The call came, and he started a church in Dover, Delaware. The Lord was with him and his wife as the ministry exploded, and now they are having three services on Sunday, ministering to several thousand. God will bless those who honor Him and trust Him. Where is this man's fifty-yard line? I have no idea. He may only be a quarter of the way down the field, or he may be closing in on the end zone of his life. Only God knows. There are many players who have come through the ranks, playing the game, finishing strong. Some have gone on to being coaches or TV sportscasters, and many have gone on to other lines of work, such as doing commercials. There are many players who were very good at what they did on the field and became coaches but failed. The Peter Principle plays out many times in life. Many souls have been lost at the fifty-yard line, and many games have been lost at the fifty-yard line when the clock ran out and the game came to an end. I pray that you will be like Paul who said, "I have run my race. I have finished my course." You can be a game changer.

CHAPTER 3

The Offensive Line

The offensive line is the one in possession of the ball, and it is their job to advance down the field to the opponent's end zone and score. The opponent will put up their best defensive line to keep you from achieving your goal. The offensive linemen primarily have one job to do, and that is to block. The line consists of the center, and he is the player who snaps the ball. But that is not all his responsibility. He blocks defensive players, calls out blocking assignments, and makes last-second adjustments to the line. There are two guards and two tackles who line up on either side of the center, and each has a specific role to play. This is where practice comes into play. There is time spent on the field, overview, class, repetition, videos, and weight room; and all are important to prepare for the game. Behind the offensive line is the balance of the team—the quarterback, running back, wide receiver, and the tight end. The quarterback is the most important position on the offensive side. He is responsible for receiving the play from the coaches and then communicating them to the players. Much of the game depends on him, yet it is an all team effort, relying on one another. The running backs are the ones who receive the ball from the quarterback and then execute a rushing play. The wide receivers are specialists who run different routes to get open for a pass. The tight ends are those who can play different positions. Sometimes they may block, and other times, they may catch passes.

How about we take a look at this from a Christian-life viewpoint? Once you are born again, you are no longer your own. You have been bought with a price. You are a new creature in Christ Jesus. Old things are past, and behold, all things have become new. You may not see any change immediately, but it will take place if you are serious with God. The inward man is being renewed day by day. So how do you play this game of life now that you have been changed? First, it is a team effort. You are not in it by yourself. There are coaches, trainers, captains, and other team players there with you. How much time have you spent with God today? Are you spending time alone with Him or in a group setting? Do you listen to His still small voice, or are you so busy talking that you can't hear Him when He is speaking? How much time are you spending in the rule book? I know many who will spend an hour or two per day just communing with God. They are listening as well as asking questions and letting their request be made known to God. Bible studies are always a good way to share and learn in a group. Many churches have left this to a pastor, but he cannot do it all. Within a group, you may find that there are those who pray with results. There are others who will support you and hold you up when you feel weak. You will find that Jesus is never more than a breath away because He said that He would never leave you or forsake you. He sticks closer than a brother. Your "center" may be your spouse or a close friend who wants you to take charge in the home or in a group. Your guards may be your unseen angels blocking the fiery darts of the enemy. We all have ministering angels, and they stand ready to perform God's Word. I know a man who started his walk of faith in God through the encouragement of his neighbor who supplied him with books and tapes of people who not only talked the talk but also walked the walk. We all need mentors, and for this man, they were Kenneth and Gloria Copeland, Jessie Deplantis, Kenneth Hagin, Jerry Seville, Charles Capps, Norvel Hayes, John Osteen, and Smith Wigglesworth. This same man saw his son healed instantly by the Word of God's power. Life and death are in the power of the tongue. We need to watch out, for what we say may come back to us. Role-playing is always a good way to practice. With football, half the team will be offensive, and the other half will play defensive. We don't know when we will cross our fifty-yard line, so we need to approach each day as if it is now. Jimmy Hoppa shared that as he was leaving the fairgrounds. After giving out Bibles, he said, "Just one more soul for Jesus." And on his way out, he had the opportunity to give his last Bible to a child. He was like the wide receiver that day, catching the pass and delivering.

The quarterback is the most important position on the offensive line. Many times, he is the one who makes things happen when there seems to be no way. He needs to be aware of what is happening around him as well as what is happening downfield. He calls the plays that he receives from the coaches on the sideline, and there are times when adjustments need to be made in a split second. He is responsible. For one who is going on a mission trip, plans are made in advance by a leader who knows the area. Everything rests on his shoulders to make sure that it is a successful trip. Those who will be hosts and lodging along with food and travel are all planned in advance of the trip. The cost is also calculated in the event that a fundraiser needs to be conducted, and that needs to be managed as well. Everyone going on the trip has a specific job to do, and some may even do more than one like the wide receiver in football. These receivers are specialists at what they do, yet there are times when they may be called on to block.

The two guards who line up on either side of the center have a specific job, and that is to block in both running and passing plays. They must be ready to pull in the event of plays known as traps (inside runs) or sweeps (outside runs) or screens (passing plays). For the Christians, this would be those who are in their "war room" (prayer closet), praying fervently for you as you go through battles of your own, lifting you up to God for protection and guidance. As we look through the scriptures, we see that Paul prayed for the saints continually, even making mention of them by name as we see in Philemon 1:4. The guards are always ready to do all they can to take care of their teammates as they move the ball downfield. Many of the ladies in our church pray daily and continually for those in need in the body of Christ.

The two tackles play outside the guards, and their job is to block and protect the quarterback. These are those in the church who know the Word of God and put the Word with all its power up as a wall against the enemy. I think of various people in our church who are constantly in prayer. M's Louise, one of the older saints in the body of Christ, prays daily for the members of our church, making remembrance of them in her prayer time. And then there is M's Elaine who not only spends time in prayer but is also able to visit those who cannot get out, providing not only food but also fellowship. Others, such as these ladies, stand in the gap, putting up a wall against the onslaught of the opponents. These are the ones who seldom get recognition for all that they do. And yet the scriptures tell us in Hebrews 12:1 that "We are surrounded by so great a cloud of witnesses, let us lay aside every weight and the sin which so easily ensnares us and let us run with endurance the race that is set before us..." These are the ones who run the race on their knees daily.

The tight end can be either a wide receiver or an offensive lineman depending on the situation, and because they are eligible receivers, they can catch passes. The scripture tells us in 2 Timothy 4:2 to be ready in and out of season. Have you ever found yourself in a situation where you wanted to share your faith with someone and suddenly you were interrupted? What do you do? You change from being a wide receiver to being an offensive lineman. Do you leave Scripture with the one who you were about to share with, or do you leave with the hope to come back? Maybe we need to listen to the words of Kenny Rogers, "You got to know when to hold 'em, know when to fold 'em, know when to walk away, and know when to run. You never count your money when you're sittin' at the table, there'll be time enough for countin' when the dealing's done." So many churches are wrapped up in numbers of attendees that they forget about souls saved for Jesus. It is not just the pastor's job to win the lost but also for every one of the believers to do their part in sharing with a lost and dying world the love of God and therefore win the lost too. Our head coach, Jesus, said, "Go into the entire world and preach the gospel to everyone." One of the ways is by word of mouth, and the other is by your actions. Many times, we open our mouths too soon when it would have been better to show someone the love of God rather than tell them.

I knew someone many years ago who teamed up with another person to go cold calling to sell insurance. They hadn't had much success, so after lunch, they decided to change their game plan. Instead of asking people if they wanted to buy any life insurance, they started by letting people know who they were and that they were not there to sell them any life insurance because they did not have the time that day. More sales were made in the afternoon than in the morning on that day. There are times when you just have to make adjustments in how you approach the play. Some plays are made straightforward, while others are cross field and down the opposite side. The fifty-yard line doesn't move in the game of football. Only the line of scrimmage moves, and this is based on ten-yard increments. This line, hopefully, tells you how much ground you have gained; however, it can also tell you how much ground you have lost. They say that you can eat a whole elephant one bite at a time. So if you set short-range goals of ten yards at a time and achieve them, then you will get to the finish line. Christians, like football players, should set short-range goals for themselves. If you are trying to memorize a scripture, don't pick the longest but the shortest to begin with. Build your way up gradually through memorizing longer verses and then segments and then chapters. The longest for me has been Psalm 91 through verse 4 of Psalm 92. Jack Van Impe was probably the most renowned for scripture memorization with several thousand put to memory. He ran his race and finished his course on January 18, 2020, at the age of eighty-nine. He reached the end zone of his life.

The fifty-yard line of life changes almost daily, and we see this with the coronavirus now changing our world as we knew it to something we never thought would happen in our lifetime. Lives are being changed instantly either by death or by daily routines or finances. This is the time when many politicians use a catastrophe to blame someone else for their own shortfalls. There will always be someone to blame until you take a good hard look in the mirror. You really never know when your game is over until it is over, so you keep playing because you have other team members relying on you and a head coach who called you to play. 1 Peter 2:9 says, "You are a chosen generation, a royal priesthood, a holy nation, His own special people, that you may proclaim the praises of Him who called you out of darkness into His marvelous light." It is very important to know who you are in Christ Jesus and the position you have been called to play. Paul writes in the Epistle to the Ephesians in chapter 4, "And He Himself gave some to be apostles, some prophets, some evangelists, and some pastors and teachers, for the equipping of the saints for the work of ministry, for the edifying of the body of Christ…" We all are given a job to do, and many have more than one job.

I find that if we spend more time perfecting our job and our skills, we spend less time finding fault with other players and the job they are doing. There are times when we need to just humble ourselves in the sight of God, not learn how to do a new victory dance or backflip or side bump with a buddy like they do in professional football, all for the cameras, but let the Lord lift us up. Therefore, let us remember this from the book of Colossians: "Whatever you do in word or deed, do all in the name of the Lord Jesus, giving thanks to God the Father through Him." Your fifty-yard line may have just extended downfield.

CHAPTER 4

The Defensive Line

The defensive team does not have possession of the ball, and their objective is to keep the other team from scoring. They do this by forcing a turnover of the ball. This happens when the offensive team runs out of time and has not completed a ten-yard gain at the end of three downs. They are forced to punt on the fourth down. They may also be forced to give up the ball through a fumble or throw an interception. You don't know what is going to happen once you go out on the field to play, but whatever happens, you need to be prepared to make adjustments. The defensive team will do all they can to keep you from reaching your goal, from scoring, and from having success. They will hit you with all they have and will not be relentless in giving you a battle. The rules are nonrestrictive to the defensive team in most situations. A defensive player can line up anywhere on his side. So let's take a look at this from a Christian viewpoint in the game of life. The defensive team is the world, and their intention is to keep you from fulfilling your calling. The players are fallen angels, and they use the world to stop the Christians from advancing the kingdom of God. When Christians take a stand for the Word of God and refuse to give into the world's way of compromise, the defense will use the courts to disrupt a way of life, to bankrupt the Christian, and to make their way unbearable to the best of their ability. We saw that happen with a husband and wife who are Christians and who owned a bakery business. Taking a stand for their convictions, they lost it all for the sake of a wedding cake. With all the bakeries in the area, they were targeted because of their Christian beliefs. The rules that are applied to one team are not always applied to the other. So let us now take a look at the various players and their positions.

The defensive backs, also known as secondaries, are primarily used to defend against pass plays. They may also attempt to intercept the pass or just keep the play from taking place. The defensive backs are also the last line of defense along with the safeties on running plays and are able to make open-field tackles. Let's take a look at this from another viewpoint. Say, the story of Samson and Delilah. He's the one who had the hair that had never been cut, and she is the one who tried to entice him to tell her the secret of his strength. He destroyed his opponents at every turn. He reminds of a player they called the Refrigerator who played for the Bears. He was big and strong, and not many, if any, got passed him. Well, Delilah was approached by the Philistine lords to inquire where his strength came from and what needs to be done to overpower him. They were willing to pay her a large sum of money for the answer. Like many journalists today, they kept coming and pressing for an answer that suited them. He kept dodging and swerving from the left to the right and back again, not giving them the answer they wanted. Until finally, after much pestering, he told her all that was in his heart. You see, the journalists, like the Philistine lords and the defensive backs, focused on the one making the play, and they set out to destroy him.

The cornerbacks attempt to prevent quarterbacks from successfully completing a pass by knocking it down or intercepting the ball themselves. If they are in a rushing situation, their job changes to stopping the runner from advancing the line of scrimmage. Going back to the story of Samson, after they cut off his hair and his strength was gone, they put his eyes out. At this point, his advancement against the Philistines had ended. They put him to forced labor, doing whatever they wanted him to do. Your opponents will stop at nothing to keep you from advancing, so you keep moving your fifty-yard line. Over time, his hair grew back. The Philistines decided to have a huge party over their accomplishment and how they had destroyed their opponent, and it was during this time that Samson was brought in to perform for all of them. He felt for the pillars that held up the building, called on God for his strength one more time, and pushed on the pillars until they collapsed, killing every one of his opponents. Only God knows when your game is over. The game is not over until the clock runs out. Is there still time on your clock? Are there plays that still need to be made? Have you fulfilled your calling?

The safeties are the final line of defense and farthest from the line of scrimmage. They are usually larger and stronger and provide extra protection on running plays. There is also a free safety who is usually smaller and faster of the two. He plays deeper on the defense for the long passes.

Rather it be defensive tackles, defensive ends, linebackers, cornerbacks, or safeties, they all have a job to do; and that is to keep you from doing yours. And so it is in the game of life. As you move or struggle to reach your fifty-yard line, the opponents will come out against you, and they have special teams that may also be called to help them accomplish their mission. We saw this back in the sixties when one person was offended by prayers in school, and she called on the ACLU (American Civil Liberties Union) and others, even the Supreme Court, to remove prayers and the Bible from our schools. Millions upon millions of students have lost the opportunity to learn how our founding fathers relied on the Bible as they formed our constitution and the part that it played in the foundation of our nation. Without a strong foundation in the family and our nation, we will continue to see prisons overflowing and the order of things being disrupted. So yes, there are special teams that will be called upon to disrupt, maim, or destroy your way of life. However, as Christians, we also have a special team who is more powerful, more knowledgeable, and more all-knowing than any special team the world has. Our team is made up of God the Father, Jesus the Son, and the Holy Spirit. They have *never* been defeated and *never* will be. In the book of Daniel, he speaks of the Ancient of Days, saying, "Until the Ancient of Days came, and a judgement was made in favor of the saints of the

Most High and the time came for the saints to possess the kingdom." God was and is and forever will be. John tells us about Jesus that "In the beginning was the Word and the Word was with God and the Word was God. He was in the beginning with God. ALL things were made through Him and without Him nothing was made that was made." Jesus spoke of the helper that He would guide us in *all* truth because the Spirit is truth. (John 16:7, 16:13 and 1 John 5:6)

There are codes for the defensive formations that indicate the number of players at each position, such as the 3-4 defense and the 4-3. The first number being the number of defensive linemen, and the second number refers to the number of linebackers. We also see codes used by various people or activists to stir the people into action, such as shutting down highways or government buildings. As Christians, we need to be alert at all times, sensitive to the Holy Spirit when He talks with us and gives us direction. He will not have us disrupt our government or its operation, but He will call us to our prayer room or war room. There are codes to get into office buildings, bank vaults, car doors, computers, houses, phones, offices, etc. There is a code to be used when entering your prayer room (war room), and that code is spelled J-E-S-U-S for He said in John 14:14, "If you ask anything in My name, I will do it." Over the years, I have seen many people protected from serious injury just by calling out that name. There is also another code word—*say*. According to Mark 11:23, Jesus speaking, "For assuredly, I say to you, whoever SAYS to this mountain, Be removed and be cast into the sea and does not doubt in his heart, but believes that those things he SAYS will be done, he will have whatever he SAYS."

CHAPTER 5

Special Teams

There are units called special teams used during a kicking play, and some of the players may be from the offensive or defensive squad who will perform their same duties. However, there are those who are specialists in their field. Here are few:

1. placekicker or pastor: The placekicker is the one who handles the kickoffs and the field goal attempts. There is a tee used when the game is starting or after a team has scored a touchdown, and they kick to the other team. During a field goal attempt, there is no tee used, but the ball is positioned by the holder.

Just like the placekicker, the pastor, most times, gets the game going. Many churches have altar calls after a message that should stir the heart and bring about conviction of sin in one's life, at least the more traditional churches (many churches have done away with the altar call). Some of these churches are about making someone feel good and not bringing them under conviction of their sin problem. This game of life is serious, and at the end, you will spend eternity in one of two places. The pastor is held more accountable than anyone else in the church, and they will be rewarded accordingly. They are responsible for their flock. I guess this is why they take a head count each Sunday to see if there are ninety-nine or one hundred. Do they have to go out and look for the lost, or are all accounted for?

2. holder/apostles: The holder is positioned about eight yards back from the line of scrimmage, and he holds the ball for the placekicker. This position is very important because if he does not place the ball in the exact position for the kicker, the ball could go to the right or left of where it needs to be.

The apostle, like the holder, has a job to do on the mission field. He shares the gospel and initiates a great moral reform and advocates an important belief to a region. He checks up on what is happening around the region to see if anyone is bringing disgrace on the church by their actions or deeds. He appoints people who are qualified to handle certain positions within the body of Christ. They need to meet certain standards.

3. Long snapper/evangelist: The long snapper is a center who specializes in snapping the ball directly to the holder or punter. He is different from the regular center who places the ball in the quarterback's hand because he has to snap the ball much farther back on kicking plays.

The evangelist is a layman who preaches at special services, such as when the pastor is away from the pulpit for meetings or vacation or due to sickness. They may also fill in when others are not available for services elsewhere. Many who are called into the position of evangelist go, as they are led by the Holy Spirit into foreign countries and areas where the gospel has never been heard.

4. punter/prophets: The punter drops the ball from their hand and kicks it while in the air. This happens when one team relinquishes possession to the defensive team. The turnover is done on the fourth down after the offensive

team has done all they can to move the ball downfield but not able to complete the mission.

The prophet is given to the church body to uplift, and encourage the church family in their daily walk with Christ.

5. punt returner/teachers: The punt returner is responsible for catching kicked balls and running the ball back as far downfield as they can get. Normally they are the fastest runners on a team.

The teachers are responsible for teaching the Word of God by equipping the body of Christ with scripture for daily use, rightly dividing the word of truth, "Edifying the body of Christ until we all come to the unity of the faith and of the knowledge of the Son of God, to a perfect man, to the measure of the stature of the fullness of Christ; that we should no longer be children, tossed to and fro and carried about with every wind of doctrine." The deeper things of God are for those who are of full age, according to the book of Hebrews 5:14. "But solid food belongs to those who are of full age, that is, those who by reason of use have their senses exercised to discern both good and evil." However, according to Hebrews 5:12–13, "There are those who should be teachers by now and yet need someone to teach them again the first principles of the oracles of God; and you have come to need milk and not solid food. For everyone who partakes only of milk is unskilled in the word of righteousness, for he is a baby."

6. Upback/gift of the word of wisdom/faith/gift of healing: The upback is a blocking back who makes the calls and guards the punter. He is the last line of defense for the punter.

There are various people within the body of Christ whom the Holy Spirit has given gifts to. He gives to each person one or more gifts as He chooses. The word of wisdom may be used in a specific setting, such as a one-on-one situation. There is a gift of faith when one walks on a path that others refuse or are fearful of. There is also a gift of healing. Jesus said, "That we shall lay hands on the sick and they shall recover." This happens when someone has the gift of healing operating through them so the other person can receive it. I know of a man who spoke to the hailstorm, and all his property was protected even though the hail came down all around him and did extensive damage. I know of a man who laid hands on someone, and they were healed of a rotator cuff injury. I know of a man who laid hands on his son, and he was healed of dehydration.

7. gunner/gift of the word of knowledge/gift of tongues: The gunner is a player who is very quick on his feet and who specializes in getting downfield after a kickoff or punt in an attempt to tackle the kick returner or punt returner.

The word of knowledge comes at a time when it is needed most to show not only that God is aware of what is going on in someone's life but also that He will take care of the situation. The gift of tongues is something that not every Christian agrees on. Paul wrote and addressed this subject several times and even stated that "I wish you all spoke in tongues." Like the gunner, we need to be swift on our feet. When the enemy comes against you unexpectedly, sidestep and start praying in the spirit. Paul understood the importance of being able to pray in the spirit, and he also knew of the importance of praying with the understanding. Paul, as he was led by the Holy Spirit, wrote to the people in Corinth concerning this matter. His first letter to the Corinthians on chapter 14 and verses 13 and 14 makes it very clear that if he prays in tongues, it is his spirit that prays, but his natural man does not know what his spirit man is saying. The devil may get into your head where the natural man is and may mess with your mind. However, he cannot get into your spirit where the Spirit of God is. So I find myself praying in tongues.

There are also prayer warriors who are always ready and are praying without ceasing. These are often the ones you never hear about, receive no recognition, and most often not distinguishable in a crowd. They are the front line, possibly standing on your fifty-yard line, calling on God and His word to empower you and propel you forward as you move through life from day to day. Many prayer chains have been set up as a cord through the family of God, most by phone and now through the World Wide Web and texting. More people can be reached now than ever before in history within seconds. I do wonder sometimes how many prayers are actually heard and answered when there is no agreement. Jesus said, "That where two or three are gathered together in My name and agree, I am in the midst of you."

CHAPTER 6

Essential Personnel

With all sports, there is what I call essential personnel. These are the people who get very little, if any, recognition, yet they are vital to the game.

Let's first take a look at the various striped shirts that are on the field and their duties.

1. referee: He is the crew chief/overseer and wears the white cap. He signals all fouls or counts the offensive players on the field and is the final authority.
2. umpire: He watches for holding and blocking or marks off penalty yardage and also counts the offensive players on the field.
3. down judge: He oversees the line of scrimmage or directs the chain crew and watches for offside and encroachment. He also rules on sideline plays and informs the referee of downs.
4. line judge: He watches for offside and encroachment or counts the offensive players on the field and rules on sideline plays.
5. field judge: He watches the receiver for illegal use of the hands and blocking fouls. He also watches for penalties on

the defensive back or watches the sidelines if a player goes out of bounds and counts the defensive players.

6. side judge: He is the primary timekeeper. He backs up the official clock operator or counts the number of defensive players on the field and signals the referee when time expires at the end of the quarter.

7. back judge: His job is to focus on the tight end and the actions around him, and he is responsible for players on the end of the lines. He keeps track of the 40- or 25-second game clock and all the TV breaks.

There is also a chain crew, and these men are responsible for moving the ten-yard chain up and down the field, depending if there was a gain or loss of yardage. They need to be precise in their marking of the ball because one inch can make the difference between a first down and a fourth down. The job of the chain crew is essential because the game can be won or lost by where the ball is placed.

There are those who carry water onto the field during a time-out to replenish the fluids lost during a game. These people are referred to as water boys. Their job is essential because they keep the players from passing out on the field due to dehydration.

Athletic trainers are the go-between for physicians and athletes and physicians and coaches. It takes dedication, skill set, and character to be an athletic trainer, and their day begins long before the actual game. The training room, where injured players will start showing up early, is prepped by having plenty of ice on hand. The trainer works with the players by stretching out their injuries and getting ready for conditioning training. Then it was down to the field where various players, depending on their injuries, started working out. Some players would run stadium steps, some would jog around the field, and others would do minor exercises in order to ensure they were staying active. Knowledge of sports medicine is important and a must for any athletic trainer. They are committed to rehabilitation of injuries from musculoskeletal injuries, sprains of ankles, and surgically repaired knees and shoulders. The learning process comes when there is an injury that they have never seen before. The challenge comes in evaluating the injury and on how to properly rehabilitate that injury. The trainer may develop new preventive programs. The trainers are required to document all injuries and rehab notes, and they are responsible for maintaining the emergency response equipment—oxygen tanks, spine boards, blood pressure cuffs, etc. The role of the athletic trainer in the athletics department is to manage the well-being of the student athlete. The job of a trainer is so much more than just tape and ice athletes.

There are essential personnel all throughout the Bible, and one story comes to mind concerning Moses and the battle with the Amalekites recorded in Exodus 17:11–13. Moses went up on the top of the hill, and as long as he held up the rod of God in his hand, Israel was winning. The day was long. Moses's arms grew weary, and as they came down, the battle shifted from Israel winning to the Amalekites winning. Aaron and Hur, two essential personnel who were with Moses, sat him on a stone and supported his hands, one on each side of Moses. His hands were steady until the sun went down. So Joshua defeated the Amalekites.

We find Peter in the book of Acts, surrounded by about one hundred and twenty, talk about a support team who cast lots for another to take Judas's place. These were all essential personnel on the day of Pentecost to bring people to repentance with a total of about three thousand souls. We also find in the upper room, by name, Peter, James, John, Andrew, Philip, Thomas, Bartholomew, Matthew, James the son of Alphaeus, Simon the Zealot, and Judas the son of James.

Who would ever think that a harlot named Rahab would be considered essential? And yet she was. We find her and her story in the book of Joshua as she saved the spies from being caught, giving victory to Israel. She gave birth to Boaz who married Ruth who gave birth to Obed the father of Jesse the father of David who became king, and if you follow the linage, you will see Jesus the Messiah twenty-eight generations later.

Paul, who wrote most of the New Testament, is definitely on the list and near the top of essential personnel. He traveled throughout Asia and from Jerusalem to Galatia and Macedonia with many traveling companions sharing the gospel of Jesus Christ. Essential personnel were left in every town where he went to carry on the work that was started, and they went from house to house. Tychicus was sent to Ephesus by Paul to share the good news, to encourage, and to comfort the brethren. Philippi had Epaphroditus, who was essential to Paul because he was sent with support from the Philippians.

In those days, there were many essential personnel who supported the ministry through prayer, material goods, and finances. An older gentleman in our church said to me one Sunday morning, "I don't have any purpose, and I'm just trying to figure out why am I still here." It really doesn't matter whether you are young or old, feeble or strong, little or big, or white, black, yellow, red, or brown. If you take the time to listen to God's voice as He speaks to your spirit in you, a whole new dimension will be opened to you in the kingdom of God. Through a kind word to a stranger, you may have shown them a new path to God. Through giving your time, you may have revealed Christ to a stranger. Through sharing your finances, you may have saved someone's family from hunger. Through praying for someone, you may have given them hope for tomorrow. Through you, the world can be a better place as you follow Christ Jesus every moment of every day. Seek Him while He can be found. Everyone in the body of Christ is *essential*.

So let's do a wrap up of all the people involved beginning with football. There are the owners, the head coach, the line coaches, and the offensive line consisting of the center, offensive guards, offensive tackles, quarterbacks, running backs, wide receivers, and tight ends. The defensive line consists of defensive tackles, defensive ends, and linebackers, which consist of the middle linebackers and the outside linebackers. And then there are the defensive backs consisting of the cornerbacks and safeties along with the nickel backs and dime backs. There are also the special teams made up of the kicker, holder, long snapper, punter, punt returner, and kick returner along with the upback and the gunner. Let us not forget the athletic trainers, the water boys, those who operate the golf cart for injuries on the field, and those who man the stretchers. There are also those in the box above the field who stay in communications with the coach on the field, calling plays. I am sure that there are some others not listed who are also essential.

The church is also made up of many players—some who are seen, and many who are unseen, behind the curtain if you will. These are the lead pastor, associate pastors, adult teachers, children teachers, researchers of materials, secretaries, money handlers, and bookkeepers along with, possibly, bodyguards. These are the custodian(s), the parking lot attendants, the ushers, the singers, and the musicians. There is also a sound crew who takes care of recordings, sound effects, volume control, and the individual microphone controls. As you can see, it takes a lot of people with talent to make a team successful and make a team function properly.

CHAPTER 7

The Game Book

The game book is not for those sitting on the sidelines or for those sitting on the bleachers, watching from a distance as the game plays out. It is for those who are in the game. John Hagee explains it very well in his book *Storm Proof*. The Bible is not a book for people sitting on the sidelines of life, watching the world go by. There are giants to fight! There are battles to win! Jesus said, "Take up your cross and follow Me." A cross is a burden to bear. It's a mission to accomplish. Every person reading this has a divine assignment. And there are going to be risks and responsibilities in making that assignment happen. It's not designed to keep you placid and uncommitted. The game book is written to give you the strategy for winning, the different formations, and what is expected from each player and their position in the game. The players are expected to read and study the game book, and of course, everyone would like to see it go off without a hitch. However, we all know that it is not that simple. There is always something or someone that causes a problem. So therefore, you have to be ready for the unexpected. That is also covered in the game book.

You must be prepared for the unexpected, have confidence in your coach, and be ready to stand your ground when called to do so. Hananiah, Shadrach, and Mishael were three among the sons of Judah who were tested when they refused to obey the king's command and turn from their God. They were ready to face death if need be rather than disobey God's command. They put all their trust on the one true God, and through the fiery furnace, He brought them out safely. Daniel was another who put his trust in his coach—the God of Abraham, Isaac, and Jacob. He refused to bow before an idol and was thrown into the lion's den. His coach brought him out safely the following morning. Then there was David who became king. He stood his ground against the giant, and he was prepared for the unexpected when he carried five additional stones in his bag. It is far better to have them and not need them than to need them and not have them. It is better to know the Word of God and have it in your heart and not need it than to not know the Word of God when you need it and not have it.

The coach makes sure that you understand the game book. He reviews it with the team and wants to know any questions. He goes over the avenues of escape from various plays that seem to be going wrong. And so it is in the game of life when things seem to be going wrong or not as you had planned it. Temptations come to draw you away from the plan book. God is faithful, who will not allow you to be tempted beyond what you are able but, with temptation, will also make the way of escape that you may be able to bear it. So we need to look at God's Word not just a book to read but also a book that we need to study and learn from. We should learn from other people's mistakes. I think that that is the hardest thing for anyone to do. How many times have we told our children "Don't do that. You'll get hurt or burned"? We see them do it anyway just to see if we are telling them the truth. Down through the ages, God has told His children what to do and how to do it. They refused to follow His game plan and missed the blessing.

Jesus was led up from the Jordan River where He was baptized into the wilderness where He was tempted by the devil. If you will take the time to read and study the scriptures, you will see that Jesus not only read the game book but also studied it. And when the devil tried to tempt Him into doing something that was contrary to the plan, He said, "IT is written." And He quoted the game book to him.

It doesn't matter what game you are playing. You need to know the plan that is laid out in the game book, and this is particularly true in the game of life. When you get to the fifty-yard line of your life, you better be prepared. The game book is always prepared in advance of the game so that the players can get their head into it. The Bible was prepared before the foundation of the world and was given to man piece by piece over centuries of time by the Holy Spirit. Exodus records that He gave Moses two tablets of the testimony, tablets of stone, written with the finger of God. Proverbs records, "Have I not written to you excellent things of counsels and knowledge?" Luke records that Jesus said our names are written in heaven. The book of Revelation records that we will be given a white stone, and on that stone, a new name, which no one knows except him who receives it, is written. I would highly recommend that you do not add to or take away from this book, for surely there are consequences. And if you want to know what they are, read Revelation 22:18–19.

I am not sure if the play book for football has chapters, but there is one thing I do know. And that is that the play book of Christians has sixty-six chapters. If this book of Books were followed, you would win every game that you played. There are dos and don'ts and what ifs. If you do the dos, you will not have to worry about the don'ts or what ifs. The scriptures tell us to be doers of the Word and not hearers only. So do what the Word says to do, say what the Word says, and walk in victory.

If a player ever tried to change the plan book, several things would or could happen. First, the coach would be very upset with the player. He may be disciplined, benched for the rest of the game, or put off the team. If a player in the game of life were to go against the game book, he may also find the same thing happen to him or her. Let's take a look in the book of Deuteronomy 28:1–2. Quote, "Now it shall come to pass, if you diligently obey the voice of the Lord your God, to observe carefully all His commandments which I command you today, that the Lord your God will set you high above all nations of the earth, and all these blessings shall come upon you and over take you, because you obey the voice of the Lord your God." The flip side begins with verse 15. Quote, "But it shall come to pass, if you do not obey the voice of the Lord your God, to observe carefully all His commandments and His statutes which I command you today, that all these curses will come upon you and overtake you." And then there is a follow-up found in the last book of Books. John wrote, under the Holy Spirit's guidance, "If anyone adds to these things, God will add to him the plagues that are written in this book; and if anyone takes away from the words of the book of this prophesy, God shall take away his part from the Book of Life, from the holy city and from the things that are written in this book." So do you see the importance of following the game book and the plan in it?

A single touchdown is not the end goal; winning with the most points is. Peace is not the end goal for the Christians; heaven is. Let's get ready for some football in the game of life. Suiting up begins in the head—having the right mental attitude to play and to win. You can't go into a game with your head wrapped around some other thoughts or distractions, such as a girlfriend, troubles at home, bills that need to be paid, problems with other teammates, etc. These obstacles can throw your game off, so get your head in the game. Then you start putting on your armor—the football shorts with built-in thigh guards and hip guards, shoulder pads, pants, and jersey along with the shoes, helmet, and mouth guard.

Paul told the Ephesians how to suit up, and this goes for all Christians who intend to get in the game. Put on the whole armor of God that you may be able to stand against the wiles of the devil. We are wrestling not against flesh and blood but against principalities, against powers, against the rulers of the darkness of this age, and against spiritual hosts of wickedness in the heavenly places. Therefore, take up the whole armor of God that you may be able to withstand in the evil day and, having done all, to stand. Gird your waist with truth (which is a clear understanding of God's Word); put on the breastplate of righteousness (which is our active obedience to the Word of God); put on your feet the preparation of the gospel of peace (which is the shalom of God); and above all, take the shield of faith (which is the complete safety by faith in the blood). No power of the enemy can penetrate the blood! With which, you will be able to quench all the fiery arrows of the evil one. Put on the helmet of salvation (which is the covering of our Lord Jesus Christ) and the sword of the Spirit (which is the Word of God; praying always with all prayer and supplication in the Spirit). Now you are ready. When your foe comes against you, he will have no mercy. Be ready. Stand your ground.

CHAPTER 8

And the Game Begins

Each game consists of four fifteen-minute quarters. Why it takes three hours to finish is beyond me, other than time spent on commercials, of which some are very funny to watch. I always liked the Budweiser commercials. There are some new ones out there, but none are as good as the Clydesdales. The rest of the time is wasted on what they call halftime entertainment. People are bouncing up and down onstage, doing lip sync and gyrations. Much of which is not suitable for young children. However, since young children are not paying the tab, they really don't matter. Once a year, they do something to honor our heroes, our vets, and our first responders.

Cheerleaders from each team are gathered on opposite sides of the field, preparing to pump up the crowd. The referee goes to the center of the field where he meets with three captains from each team on the fifty-yard line. The captains shake hands, and the visiting team gets to call the coin, either heads or tails, before it is tossed by the referee. It is an official coin used for that game. If the player calls the toss correctly, he gets to choose one of three options. The first option is which team receives the kickoff. The second option would be which goal his team will defend, and the third option is when to decide. This option could determine the outcome of the game because they may want to receive the ball on the second half rather than on the first half.

The coin is tossed. And the visiting team chooses heads, and heads it is. Meanwhile up in the stands, the fans are getting fired up for their team, and the refreshments are beginning to flow from hotdogs to peanuts to sodas and beer. Souvenirs can also be purchased from various vendors for either team. Some people get very serious about their team and come in costumes and makeup all over their faces, matching the team colors. Meanwhile out on the field, the teams are getting ready for the kickoff, and the crowd is starting to get a little crazy. Along the sidelines, you can see the defensive or offensive team along with the special team. The athletic trainer is constantly on the move, looking for any injuries that need attention. There is one hundred yards that need to be covered from one end of the field to the other in order to gain points, and it is harder than one would think.

The ball is in the air, and it is long into the end zone. The players of today aren't like the players when I grew up. The ball used to be brought out to the twenty-yard line, and now it is to the thirty-yard line. And of course, they didn't wear gloves, there was no artificial grass, and they played in rain or snow. There were no domes back then. The fans tufted it out as well. The kick returner calls for a fair catch, and the first quarter is on the way as the ball is spotted on the twenty-five-yard line. For the next fifty-five minutes, take or give a few, the two teams battle back and forth up and down the field, trying to gain points by either a touchdown or field goal attempt. The crowd goes ballistic on the player who misses catching the ball or possibly fouls another player. Time-outs are called, injured players are treated on the field before being carried off the field, plays are being reviewed, and fouls are being discussed by the referees; and that is how a fifteen-minute quarter is turned into a fifty-five-minute quarter. And let us not forget the commercials that need to be run in order to pay the salaries of players, coaches, referees, and owners. Did you ever stop and think about how much that adds up to? If you have thirty players per team (probably more) and ten coaches per team (probably more) plus the owner and then the referees (times two because there are two teams at just ten million dollars average income), well, you do the math. That is why you have a three-hour show for a one-hour game. That's the end of the first quarter, and it is break time.

The second quarter begins, and it appears to be almost a repeat of the first quarter. The ball is moved back and forth from one team and then to the other, up and down the field. Points are now starting to show up on the scoreboard as players are now able to find paths through the defensive players to get within field goal range or even make a possible touchdown. As the men gather in what is known as a huddle, the quarterback shares what the next play will be. The plays are listed on a wristband or given through the headset inside the helmet of the quarterback by a coach on the sideline. Running plays have been tried along with passing plays, and with all the great and good players on each team, it is hard to say who will win. The quarterback rarely keeps the ball to make a running play. He will pass the ball off in a lateral play to one of the running backs. There are fumbles, and there are interceptions along the way. And of course, there is always the quarterback getting sacked when there is little to no protection from the defensive ends or linebackers by the offensive guards or offensive tackles. The clock winds down, and there is a two-minute warning before the first half is finished. It is time to regroup for one last push before halftime. This warning really is not needed; however, in the game of life, it would probably be much appreciated. Halftime finally gets here, and the teams leave the field and go to the locker rooms. The players relax for a short time while the various coaches go over strategies and game plans. The time allotted for halftime is usually about fifteen minutes except for the Super Bowl, and then it could be as much as a half hour.

The Christian walk in life is a lot like football except that the fifty-yard line keeps getting moved. We really don't know where is our own fifty-yard line; however, we will know when we reach the end zone. Psalm 90:10 says, "The span of our years is seventy—or with strength, eighty—yet at best they are trouble and sorrow. For they are soon gone, and we fly away." The four quarters of football and the eighty years of life (twenty-year quarters) could be viewed as learning. In life, during the first quarter, you are learning how to walk, talk, dress yourself, and feed yourself; then come more learning from teachers over the next twelve to thirteen years—everything from spelling, reading, math, science, and history. It's like the quarterback with the headset in his helmet; thoughts, ideas, and impressions are filling your head. Those who are interested in learning and knowing more will find themselves in books and on the internet—doing research, studying, and gaining knowledge. Since none of us really know where our fifty-yard line is in life, we find ourselves, many times, just wandering around, going from job to job or church to church or, even worse, from relationship to relationship. Very few search for God's guidance. He is left out of the equation until there seems to be nowhere else to turn, and even then, they hesitate about asking a God Who is bigger than the world around them. Many are afraid to try to approach someone they cannot see, let alone talk to. However, life goes on. The second quarter of life is, most times, spent getting your career off and running, making decisions about what you want to do for the rest of your life; and again, God is left out of the equation. Many people live in a self-centered world. Everything evolves around them, and they may or may not allow others into their world. I think about the receiver who made a great catch, went into the end zone, and went into different gyrations and possibly a new dance step that he created just for this moment or possibly a new way to spike the ball, forgetting about the one who made it possible—the quarterback. It is not just a one-person game. Like basketball, it is a team thing, yet only one or two get the credit. Look at what Paul had to say to the Corinthians, "Who then is Paul and who is Apollos, but ministers through whom you believed, as the Lord gave to each one? I planted, Apollos watered, but God gave the increase. So then neither he who plants is anything, nor he who waters, but God who gives the increase. Now he who plants and he who waters are one, and each one will receive his own reward according to his own labor." Paul was in a world that involved others. He had a core of people who helped him prepare for the journeys that he took. There were those who helped pen the various letters and helped financially, and there were always the prayer warriors. These prayer warriors were men and women of faith who were willing to stay on their knees well into the midnight hour.

The third quarter is spent taking care of the family that you started. Now you learn how to juggle and wear different hats. We can take a look at Paul's life and how, at this point in his life, he looked after the churches that he started throughout the region. Many times, it would begin with one-on-one discussion and teachings of the scriptures. The group grew, as others were added daily, and a church was established. He did this from town to town across the region, and the church body was established. There were helpers who traveled with him, and as devout men grew in faith and knowledge of the Word of God, they were appointed to pastors and deacons. Like in football, we see the quarterback lateral pass to another, so Paul has done many lateral passes, not by being the pastor of any one church but by passing the duties to another. He followed up on the work that he had started by traversing back and forth across Macedonia and Galatia, down to Jerusalem and the surrounding areas. He was not only a preacher but also a tentmaker by trade. He was a teacher of the Word of God to rich and poor alike. He suffered much for the cause that he believed in as he records in 2 Corinthians 11:23–28. He became all things to all people. "In labors more abundant, in stripes above measure, in prisons more frequently, in deaths often, From the Jews five times I received forty stripes minus one, three times I was beaten with rods; once I was stoned; three times I was shipwrecked; a night and a day I was in the deep; in journeys often, in perils of waters, in perils of robbers, in perils of my own countrymen, in perils of the gentiles, in perils in the city, in perils in the wilderness, in perils in the sea, in perils among false brethren; in weariness and toil, in sleeplessness often, in hunger and thirst, in fastings often, in cold and nakedness—besides the other things, what comes upon me daily; my deep concern for all the churches." And we think that we have it bad? Maybe we need to take another look in the mirror. Many times, players are close-knit, like family with concerns for one another's well-being. Somewhere on or near the fifty-yard line of life, we find ourselves so involved in taking care of self, our spouse, and our children; and we tend to forget about our church family, the widows, widowers, and orphans—those who are hurting spiritually, financially, and physically. Our finances make themselves wings and fly away. Many times, we lose focus. Things get blurry and out of line. We go into debt to satisfy desires and wants for our family; and the need of the church is set aside for the sake of a new house or car, vacation, toys for the children, and our own toys like a boat, hunting equipment, fishing equipment, etc. However, Malachi made it very plain in chapter 3 and verse 8, "Will a man rob God? Yet you have robbed Me! But you say, 'In what way have we robbed You? In tithes and offerings.'" Solomon said in Proverbs 3:9, "Honor the Lord with your possessions and with the first fruits of ALL your increase." The third quarter of life should be spent taking care of family, not just the family under your roof but also the family of God. In today's world, again, God is left out of the equation for most families. If He can be found, He would probably be found down the ladder around the third or fourth rung. However, God has always had a remnant—those who are sold out for Him, who get so involved in His word and teachings that they go on to Bible college, and who become engaged in the ministry of sharing Christ with a lost and dying world.

In my mind's eye, I can picture the angels of God, ministering angels, assigned to be with each and every Christian—tailgating, high fiving, low fiving, and doing their strut. They are talking about the team and how they have been put to work, performing the Word. Jeremiah records God's Word, "You have seen correctly, for I am watching over My word to perform it." They are talking about the saint who was praying. Many people pray, but only a few get through. Why? Because they pray in faith, believing God's Word to be true, and they do not waiver. They talk about the receiver. Here are two different people: one who receives Christ as Savior and the other who receives answer to prayer for healing, finances, etc. The receiver of Christ gets a standing ovation with loud cheers and hallelujahs. The one who received sight or hearing or set free from demons or received a financial breakthrough and even the one who was healed of cancer gives high praises to God, and the angels rejoice. There is talk all over heaven about the one who stood in the gap when no one else could be found. Many times, there is no one found who would take a stand in the gap for a cause to protect the land. Ezekiel mentions this in his writings. However, I know a man who heard the news reports and saw the clouds gathering and the wind starting to blow, and he went out and took a stand and spoke to the wind and the storm clouds. And they broke up and became still, protecting the land. The angels are talking about the long pass that connected with a player downfield (trust God). There is talk about the runner who didn't stop and never looked back. I think of men like Billy Graham, Martin Luther, John Wesley, and Smith Wigglesworth who stayed the course and who put the world behind them and the cross before them, no turning back. There is talk of the one who can do it—make a play happen.

I think of the story from a Gideon who was distributing Bibles on a college campus. The discussion came up in one of the classrooms that Bibles were being made available outside. During the class break, the professor came out and talked with the Gideon and invited him into the next class to share who the Gideons are and what they are doing. He went in and spoke of Jesus and the plan of salvation and then handed Scriptures to everyone in the room. You see, there is rejoicing, cheering, and shouting when a sinner comes to Jesus for salvation. I find it a bit sad, however, that the church can get all excited over some athlete who just scored the winning point, yet when it comes to the saving of a soul from hell, it just gets passed over. Why is that? Could it be that we have become so earthly focused on heroes in this world that we forget about the heroes in the world to come? Many of the old saints have now left and gone on to be with Jesus. And yes, there are still many here who are fulfilling the great commission. The baton had been handed off, and these heroes are running their race as they bring comfort to those in despair, healing to those who are in need of physical and spiritual healing. They have brought the Word of God to the downtrodden and made it alive to those who were dead spiritually. They are the heroes who have been entrusted with wealth because God knows they will do right with it for the good of others.

Remember the story of the steward who was given five talents; another, given two talents; and another, given one. The first two took the talents given them and traded wisely and produced a return. However, the third servant took what little he had and did nothing with it. He returned it back to his master, and he was not happy. The servant could have at least put the one talent in the bank and gained interest, but he didn't even do that. This is why most have little or none. God wants us to use the talents He gives us for His glory. There is an old saying, "It is better to shoot at something and miss than to shoot at nothing and hit."

The quarterback who throws the long pass to where the receiver is to be is better than the one who plays it safe and just holds onto the ball. There are those who spend much time in prayer, reaching to the throne room of God and receiving their petitions. Many Christians have what is called a war room or locker room, if you like. This is where many wars are fought and won even before anyone knew that there was a battle getting ready to unfold. Many good coaches study their opponents long before they actually confront them on the field. They will watch the games played by the upcoming opponent against other teams. They will look at the various moves and plays by the players, hoping to get a heads-up before they face them on the field. It is good to get to know something about our opponent and how he operates. He will use whatever is available to distract, upset, misguide, and even destroy those who follow Christ. He will even use friends, spouses, children, coworkers, and even the boss, if necessary, to get you to say or do something that is not right. We know that he goes about as a roaring lion seeking whom he may devour. You see, he only has as much power as we allow, and that is why he is "like" a roaring lion trying to instill fear into the heart of man. Always remember this: "fear tolerated is faith contaminated."

The fourth quarter has begun. Are you still in the game, or have you given up? It saddens me to see, way too often, players just give up. They seem to be overwhelmed by the scoreboard that doesn't seem to be in their favor. Time isn't really on their side, and the fans have turned against them. Maybe one of their best players has been taken out of the game and put on the injured list. There is an old cliché, "Drop back five and punt." This is not the time to do that. Stay focused, play to win, and give it your all for the team. Remember, everyone has a position on the team, and there are times when you may have to perform two or three and perhaps four different jobs. Can you multitask? Some can, and then there are others who can't walk and chew gum at the same time. But that's okay. We all know some of those people (we may be one of them), and you know what, God can still use us.

Think about King David. He grew up taking care of sheep, not very strong like his brothers, but he had confidence in himself and his God. The time of testing came when the Philistines came out against King Saul and his army. They found themselves across the valley from one another. There was a giant of a man called Goliath who fought for the Philistines, and he would come out and taunt the Hebrews and make fun of them and their God. David was sent to bring food to his brothers and found out how the battle was going, and as he came to his brothers, he heard this loud booming voice calling to the king's army. He decided that he had enough of this and that he would go out and fight the giant. His brothers and many of the king's men laughed at him, but he was determined. So the king had him put on his armor, but it was too awkward and heavy. He took off the armor, pulled out his sling, gathered up five stones, and headed toward the giant. After listening to Goliath laugh and scorn David's God, he started running toward him and encouraged himself as he went by, saying, "I killed a bear, and I killed the lion. And today I will remove your head and feed your carcass to the birds of the air." There is an old saying, "It is not the size of the man in the fight but the size of the fight in the man." No matter your size, your skin color, or your national origin, if you have the living God in you, you can achieve anything.

Are you standing on your fifty-yard line, holding the ball that was given to you and wondering what to do with it? You have to do something or be crushed by the opposition. So why not be like David? Run at your opposition with all that is within you. Encourage yourself. The fifty-yard line is just the halfway point. You need to know that the end zone is not far-off. You can make it. Look at Jerry Rice, wide receiver for the San Francisco 49ers. He wasn't big, but he was fast. His heart was in the game. His size didn't matter. His legs didn't fail him. He pressed on and completed the majority of his missions. Many of the great quarterbacks like Johnny Unitas and John Elway would stand their ground when everything around them was falling down until the last second and would then release the ball, sending it downfield into the hands of a receiver before being taken down themselves. And so it is with those wanting to walk the path set before them as followers of Christ.

The game is not over until the clock stops. Since we cannot clearly see our own fifty-yard line, we need to be always ready to give an answer concerning the hope that is in us. We would all like to finish out our years as God has promised. However, that does not always happen. Things happen. People are careless about what they say. Many pronounce their own death sentence with saying things like, "I won't live past retirement age." "My dad and grandfather didn't live past sixty, so I probably won't either." "All my family have had heart problems, so I'm sure I will too." And here is one for you: "If that happens, I'll just die." Psalm 141:3 says, "Set a guard, O Lord, over my mouth; Keep watch over the door of my lips."

I know of a man who has a friend whose wife was given bad news by the doctor, and the man asked everyone to pray for her because the diagnosis was not good. This man prayed the Word of God with confidence toward God that she shall live and not die. Today, some fifteen years later, she is healthy and is watching her children grow up. According to the book of Proverbs 18:21, "Death and life are in the power of the tongue, and those who love it will eat its fruit." Many pastors have taught that when you pray, you should say "if it be God's will." Well, what is God's will? His will is spelled out in His Word. Jesus said, "I am the door. If anyone enters by Me, he will be saved and will go in and out and find pasture. The thief does not come except to steal and kill and destroy. I have come that they may have life and that they may have it more abundantly." And in another place, God says, "I desire that you prosper and be in good health even as your soul prospers."

Many times, some of the best players are removed from the game because of pride and making it an "I" game instead of a team game, and they are replaced by someone who is humble, not self-centered and boastful. Many ballplayers focus on maybe one or two good years to negotiate their contract and how much money they can get. Many preachers are the same way. The players get comfortable, playing good ball, yet keep negotiating higher contracts. It is all about the money. When one takes their eyes off the prize, they tend to be shortsighted. For pastors and preachers, it should always be about souls for the kingdom of God. For ballplayers, it should be for the good of the team. Paul, who was humbled before God, had a thorn in the flesh to buffet him that he would stay focused on Jesus, the Messiah. He went through many trials and hardships, yet he never lost focus on his calling to win souls for Christ.

CHAPTER 9

The Two-Minute Warning

The two-minute warning is sounded, and there is a break in the action. The coaches and players get together for one last time to discuss their strategy for coming out on top. They get their last drink of water and get back in position to finish the game. They are refreshed, pumped up, and encouraged to bring the game to a close. If every player approached the game like Paul approached the ministry and if every player approached the final two minutes like Paul approached his final hours, their game could have ended differently. Paul, knowing that chains and tribulations awaited him, said, "But none of these things move me; nor do I count my life dear to myself, so that I may finish my race with joy and the ministry which I received from the Lord Jesus, to testify to the gospel of the grace of God." Many of the football players look for just one more chance to dance, do the belly bump, or flip over backward, win or lose.

The fifty-yard line has been passed, and the ball is being moved toward the end zone. Scoring has been tough. However, first downs have been achieved, and the goalpost is in range. Only six points separate the teams. A touchdown and the point after could clinch the game. The offensive line is in the huddle, and they are given the signal. Excitement grows, and the adrenaline flows. They are ready to make the final push. Across from them is the defensive line with determination on their faces to stop any advancement. As the signal is being shouted out, men are starting to move around, and then they are set. The ball is snapped. You can hear the grunts and groans as helmets clash along with shoulder pads and muscle against muscle. One of the linebackers is determined to move through the line. The quarterback drops back as he looks for his receivers. The defensive ends are making their move to get to the quarterback, and at the same time, the linebackers are breaking through the offensive line as they keep their eye on the ball. The quarterback is now moving to the left, looking downfield for a receiver. He looks right, and just as the defensive end is closing in on him, he throws downfield to his left and into the hand of his receiver. He pulls the ball into his chest and turns to go for the touchdown. However, there is a cornerback right there, and he pushes him out of bounds. The offensive line gained five yards on the play. The second down is about to be played when time-out is called by the offensive coach. The next play is discussed, a few words of encouragement, and the quarterback returns to the huddle. They break and set themselves in a new formation, one that has only been tried in practice. It is a running play, which if all goes according to plan should get them into the end zone, tying the game. The play is called, and the ball is snapped. The quarterback does a lateral pass to the running back. He fumbles the ball at the same time a flag is thrown downfield for holding. It appears that a defensive player was charged with holding a receiver. The fumble was recovered by the offensive guard, and the second down was replayed. Two more yards were gained during the second down, and now they are into the third down and three with ten seconds left on the clock. Once again, they are lined up, the snap and the receivers crisscross, and the ball is in the air, heading toward the end zone as the receivers crisscross once again. And as the ball is coming down, the receiver propels himself out with arms stretched and pulls the ball in as he crosses the goal line. The game is now tied with two seconds left on the clock. The defensive line knows that they must hold the line and do all they can to keep the ball from being kicked. From the sideline come a placekicker and a holder. The game rests with them, either they win now or go into overtime. The game of life has no overtime. When the trumpet sounds and the call goes out, the game is over. You are either in or out. The final seconds are about to be played out, which would be great to see in slow motion. The teams line up on the line of scrimmage. The players are focused, with muscles tensed, and the ball is snapped. You can hear the clash of helmets and shoulder pads. The holder receives the ball and turns it to place in the tee as the kicker is on his approach to making contact with his foot and the ball. The defensive team is gathered in front of where the ball is to stop it or deflect it from going between the goalposts. Some of their best jumpers are now in the air, reaching with all they have to touch the ball. As the ball leaves the tee, it is going up, but is it high enough? There is a slight tip by one of the cornerbacks, and the ball is deflected slightly as it goes toward the uprights. It looks like it may just…

Do you want to be left in that position? Not knowing if you make it or not is not a good position to be in. This is a question that only you can answer. Every one of us will have or had a fifty-yard line in our lives. Where are you in the game of life? Who is your head coach? Are you in the selfie generation where it is all about you? When your game is about over, are you ready to hear your Master say, "Well done"? Then finish your game with all that you have, giving glory to the King of kings and Lord of lords. There are times when you have to make decisions in your life, big decisions as well as some small ones. Every day, you have to make decisions, from the time your eyes open and all day long. There are times when you will fumble the ball or fall. There are mountains to climb and valleys to cross. The game of life is never easy; however, if you include God in your life and seek His guidance, you can't go wrong. How much of His coaching do you want? Some are just satisfied with as little as possible, while others want more, but not too much more. And then there are those who are *all* in. There are those who like to go to the ocean and stand on the sand with the water tickling their toes. Others like to go in, but just to their knees. I have seen others go waist-deep, and others go in until the water covers their head. Once you are *all* in, it doesn't matter if the water is one inch or a thousand feet over your head. It is still over your head. Just like football, you are either all in or half in, and half in doesn't work. Many are called, but few are chosen. You may have been called to play football; you have the build and the stamina and are quick on your feet, but you lack the ability to remember the plays. You may not be chosen. So it is with God's ministry. Many have different views of the ministry. However, God looks on the heart of man to see the real you—the one inside the body, the spirit man. Will you humble yourself before God and acknowledge that you are nothing without Him? The placekicker is really dependent on the holder, for without the holder doing his job properly, the placekicker can miss his mark.

When the game is over, there is a time of rest, at least until the next game, if there is one. Has your season come to a close? The scriptures tell us, "For whatever is born of God overcomes the world. And this is the victory that has overcome the world—our faith." You see, in the game of football, everything is about winning and losing. However, in life, it is not about winning or losing but about how you played the game, because in the end, if we are born again, we all win.

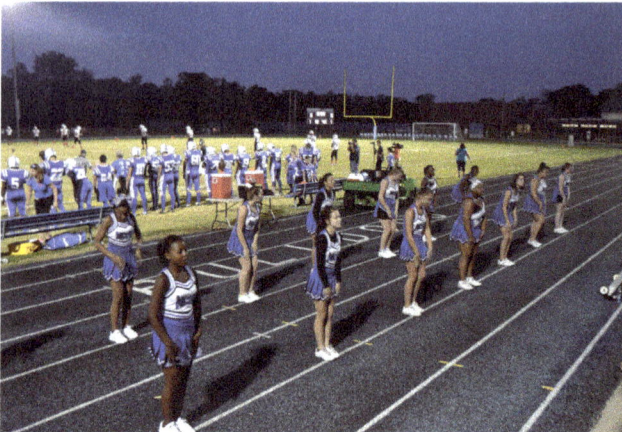

There is a person who is not thought of very often, yet he plays a very important role. He (or she) receives no recognition, no applause, no high salary, and no bonus and is, most times, taken for granted. He hustles out onto the field and hustles off, does his job, and is happy. He is the water boy. He keeps the team hydrated and water bottles full. His job is important. And so it is in the ministry. He (or she) is the one who takes care of the church behind the scenes, from bookkeeping to bulletins to phone calls and to setting appointments for the church leaders. They prepare the monthly reports, making sure that the numbers are correct, people are recognized, and meeting dates are set. Timothy was a water boy for Paul as he traveled with him, and we find later that he was promoted to caring for the church and the spreading of the gospel. There is Tychicus, who was also a "water boy" for Paul. He was sent to Ephesus to keep the people informed of the affairs of Paul and of what was taking place in the ministry and to comfort their hearts. It doesn't matter if it is a huge ministry or the local church. There will always be a need for a "water boy."

CHAPTER 10

The Homecoming

High school football, unlike the NFL (National Football League), has always had a homecoming game. This is a time when they celebrate the careers of the senior high school athletes, normally the football players. There is excitement in the air. Posters are made and placed all around the school. Some of the students decide to run for homecoming king or queen, and then ballets are cast. Most times, the winners are kept secret until game day. Clothes for the dance are decided on as the dates try to coordinate colors, maybe even school colors. This is a *big* deal. Kings and queens are chosen from the class and are crowned during halftime. They also celebrate with a homecoming dance the night after the game. The dress is more casual than for a prom—no corsages, gowns, or tux. A group may go out for a meal afterward, or there may be a meal served at the dance. Plans are, most times, made in advance so that the students as well as the parents can be prepared.

The game of life also has a homecoming celebration. Are you making plans? Have you prepared yourself for that day? I do not believe that God's kingdom is going to be a solemn, and serene place. King David made it very clear that there will be various musical instruments with singing and dancing, for he had a heart after God's own heart. The book of Psalm expresses King David's joy. Psalm 71:22–23, "Also with the lute I will praise You—And Your faithfulness, Oh my God! To You I will sing with the harp, O Holy One of Israel. My lips shall greatly rejoice when I sing to You, and my soul, which You have redeemed." 2 Samuel 6:16 records that King David was leaping and whirling before the Lord. In Psalm 150:1–6, King David tells us to praise the Lord; praise Him with the sound of the trumpet; praise Him with the lute and the harp; praise Him with the timbrel and dance; and praise Him with stringed instruments, flutes, and cymbals. Let everything that has breath praise the Lord!

The overcomers of this world are those who have been born again. These are the ones who, according to 1 John 5:4, are born of God, and this is the victory that has overcome the world—our faith. We do not get any older. Oh, our outward man will, but the inward man is renewed day by day (1 Corinthians 4:16). Because you are a spirit being, you are eternal. As one preacher said many years ago, "We are living in a space suit designed for living on earth; however, one day, we will take off this suit and receive a heavenly body. What a great HOMECOMING!" Solomon wrote, "He brought me to the banqueting house, and His banner over me was love." Homecoming is going to be so overwhelming that you can't begin to imagine. Well, how did you get to be an overcomer? You overcome the devil (the accuser) by the blood of the Lamb and by the word of your testimony. King David said that in God's presence is fullness of joy and at His right hand are pleasures forevermore. There is a great reward waiting for those who fear the Lord and call on His name. His favor is for life; weeping may endure for a night, but joy comes in the morning. There is a great shout during a football game when the home team scores a touchdown. And you can take this to the bank: there will be a joyful shout to the Lord when we all get to heaven. We will come before His presence with singing and enter His gates with thanksgiving and into His courts with praise. How many times has someone called out when they are at their fifty-yard line, saying, "O my God, do not take me away in the midst of my days"? His word is settled in heaven, and He will not relent. You will have no shame there; instead, you will have double honor, and everlasting joy shall be yours. *All* the gold and *all* the silver is the Lord's.

King Solomon was the richest man to ever live. He had it all. Anything he imagined, he got. He made a house for the Lord and overlaid everything in it with gold, yet he didn't even come close to what God has and what He has prepared for you. John the Baptist cried out, "Repent, for the kingdom of heaven is at hand!" We don't know when we will cross our goal line or if we are just approaching the fifty-yard line. But there is one thing we do know, and that is that the kingdom of God is coming. Will these words be spoken to you:

"Well done, good and faithful servant; you were faithful over a few things. I will make you ruler over many things. Enter into the joy of the Lord"? There is a lot of joy at a football game, but there is also some sorrow because there is a winner and a loser. However, there is all joy in heaven for one sinner who repents.

There is a place that is being prepared especially for you and me, and we have that assurance through scripture. Jesus was speaking, "Let not your heart be troubled; you believe in God, believe also in Me. In My Father's house are many mansions; if it were not so, I would have told you. I go to prepare a place for you and if I go and prepare a place for you, I WILL come again and receive you to Myself; that where I am, there you may be also. And where I go you know and the way you know." We have a hope that is laid up for us in heaven, where the whole family is. There you will find joy and peace like you have never experienced before in this life. Your fifty-yard line may be where you are right now, or you could have passed it long ago. Just be sure that you are ready to cross the goal line of life. Once crossed, there is no looking back.

There is an inheritance that is undefiled and that does not fade away, reserved for you in heaven. Have you ever inherited anything from someone, maybe a dad or mom or uncle, possibly an aunt or even a friend? The things that are of this world will lose their luster, decay, or just fade away and will be replaced by something else. The genuineness of your faith is what gives you hope that God is more than able to keep what He has reserved for you in heaven. Believing, you rejoice with joy inexpressible and full of glory, receiving the end of your faith—the salvation of your soul.

Have you ever tried to count the grains of sand on the seashore? No? Don't bother to try. No one can, and so it is with us who are surrounded by so great a cloud of witnesses. We should set aside every weight and sin that easily ensnares us and should run with endurance the race that is set before us. Focus on Jesus (the author and finisher of our faith) who, for the joy that was set before Him, endured the cross, despising the shame, and has sat down at the right hand of the throne of God. There is a time of rest, and Jesus (Yeshua) has entered that rest because His work on earth was completed at the cross when He said, "It is finished" and then gave up His spirit.

Have you ever purchased a new vehicle, one fresh from the assembly line that no one has owned or rented from Avis? It is all yours—no smell of cigarettes, cigars, or perfume—with a fresh scent like the scent after a summer rain. That is the way your new home in heaven will be—fresh, no previous owners, no Pine-Sol smell but freshness. God knows your likes and dislikes, so all the furnishings will be designed with you in mind. The old earth and heaven will be gone, and there will be a new heaven and a new earth. Think about that for a while. There will be no more pollen, ragweed, poison ivy, poison oak, or weeds to pull. There will be no thorns or needles to pull out of your finger. The holy city, the New Jerusalem, will come down from heaven from God, for He will make everything new. God will wipe away every tear from our eyes; there will be no more death, nor sorrow nor crying. There will be no more pain, for the former things have passed away. He makes *all* things new. And He will give of the fountain of the water of life freely to him who thirsts. The one who overcomes shall inherit all things and shall be called a son of God. There will be no place for the cowardly, unbelieving, abominable, murderers, sexually immoral, sorcerers, idolaters, and all liars; for they will have their part in the second death, which is in the lake that burns with fire and brimstone.

The holy Jerusalem is a huge city, the likes of which cannot be described nor comprehended by man. All the great castles and mansions built by man cannot compare or even hold a candle to this great city. The height and width and length were 12,000 furlongs, each furlong equaling to 220 feet for a total of 2,640,000 feet. *If* you are familiar with the construction of a house, you know that it has to have a foundation and walls. The walls are of jasper, and the city is pure gold, like clear glass. The foundations of the wall are adorned with all kinds of precious stones—the first foundation being jasper; the second, sapphire; the third, chalcedony; the fourth, emerald; the fifth, sardonyx; the sixth, sardius; the seventh, chrysolite; the eighth, beryl; the ninth, topaz; the tenth, chrysoprase; the eleventh, jacinth; and the twelfth, amethyst. The twelve gates were of pearl, one pearl for each gate. The street of the city is pure gold, like transparent glass. Are you getting a glimpse of this homecoming yet? Are you able to picture it in your mind?

There is no need for a temple in the city, for the Lord God Almighty and the Lamb are its temple. The glory of God illuminates the city, and the Lamb is its light. There will be no night there. And there is a pure river of water of life, clear as crystal, proceeding from the throne of God and of the Lamb. The tree of life is in the middle of its street and on either side. The tree of life bore twelve fruits, each tree yielding its fruit every month. There will be no night there and no need for a lamp nor light of the sun. The Lord God gives light. This homecoming will be like none other, for no eye has seen and no ear has heard all the splendors awaiting those who overcome.

If you are midway through your game, finding yourself on your own fifty-yard line of life, what are your plans to finish strong? Will you stay the course that is set before you with your face to the wind? Or will you find yourself, of course, blown by every wind of doctrine, not grounded in the Word of God? You need to settle it once and for all. Who is the owner of your team, and who is the captain whom you will follow? There remains a rest for the people of God. For he who has entered His rest has himself also ceased from his works as God did from His. If you want to come to the homecoming, you need to have a ticket to get in. If you received the ticket that Jesus made available, you can come in. The ticket is free to those who receive Jesus, no cost on your part.

There is a defensive and offensive aspect to the life of faith. Defensively, we need to be on guard against false teaching and the behavior that can result from it. Offensively, believers need to contend, applying the same discipline to their spiritual lives as the athletes do in preparing for the game (taken from the *Messianic Jewish Family Bible*).

Well, my friend, have you taken a good hard look at your life? Who is your coach? Who owns the team that you are playing for? What position do you play? Have you been called to be the quarterback, the halfback, the running back, or possibly the water boy? No matter what your position is, do it with all that is in you, and your day of rest is around the corner. Fifty-yard line or end zone, where are you?

ABOUT THE AUTHOR

The author grew up telling stories on the street corners with friends. He graduated from Catonsville High School and joined the Army National Guard. He entered the insurance industry as an agent and got married the same year. The author started to write letters to the editor, and the content got transformed into books. He first published a book in September 2010, and the second book was published in 2013. Inspired by God, the title *Life at the Fifty-Yard Line* came to him.

CPSIA information can be obtained
at www.ICGtesting.com
Printed in the USA
JSHW011139270521
15265JS00002B/4

9 781636 308401